Mimicking Nature

Heather E. Schwartz

✳ Smithsonian

Contributing Author

Jennifer Lawson

Consultants

Gary Krupnick, Ph.D.
Department of Botany
Ecologist and Evolutionary Biologist
National Museum of Natural History

Sharon Banks
3rd Grade Teacher
Duncan Public Schools

Publishing Credits

Rachelle Cracchiolo, M.S.Ed., *Publisher*
Conni Medina, M.A.Ed., *Managing Editor*
Diana Kenney, M.A.Ed., NBCT, *Content Director*
Véronique Bos, *Creative Director*
Robin Erickson, *Art Director*
Michelle Jovin, M.A., *Associate Editor*
Mindy Duits, *Senior Graphic Designer*
Smithsonian Science Education Center

Image Credits: p.11 CAIA IMAGE/Science Source; p.16 (bottom) Susumu Nishinaga/Science Source; pp. 16–17 Jackie Huang, Maurice Hampton, Bailey Beatt and Samantha Scheib with Professors Andrew Scarpelli and Heather Dewey-Hagborg; p.18 zaferkizilkaya / Shutterstock.com; p.20 NASA/JPL-Caltech; p.23 (both) Eijiro Miyako; p.25 Pascal Goetgheluck/Science Source; p.26 Kyodo/Newscom; all other image Shutterstock and/or iStock.

Library of Congress Cataloging-in-Publication Data

Names: Schwartz, Heather E., author.
Title: Mimicking nature / Heather E. Schwartz.
Description: Huntington Beach, CA : Teacher Created Materials, [2019] | Audience: K to grade 3. | Includes index. |
Identifiers: LCCN 2018030486 (print) | LCCN 2018031770 (ebook) | ISBN 9781493869152 | ISBN 9781493866755
Subjects: LCSH: Inventions--Juvenile literature. | Technological innovations--Juvenile literature. | Nature--Juvenile literature.
Classification: LCC T48 (ebook) | LCC T48 .S416 2019 (print) | DDC 609--dc23
LC record available at https://lccn.loc.gov/2018030486

Smithsonian

© 2019 Smithsonian Institution. The name "Smithsonian" and the Smithsonian logo are registered trademarks owned by the Smithsonian Institution.

Teacher Created Materials

5301 Oceanus Drive
Huntington Beach, CA 92649-1030
www.tcmpub.com
ISBN 978-1-4938-6675-5
© 2019 Teacher Created Materials, Inc.
Printed in Malaysia
Thumbprints.21251

Table of Contents

Playing with Plants 4

Growing Greenery 6

Familiar Sights.................................10

Beyond Everyday Life 16

Helping Each Other........................ 22

Partnering with Plants....................... 26

STEAM Challenge 28

Glossary.. 30

Index... 31

Career Advice 32

Playing with Plants

Have you ever climbed a tree? Have you used a stick to draw in the dirt? Have you blown fluff off a dandelion? If so, you know how to think like an **engineer**. You know how to use plants in new and different ways. A tree can be a jungle gym. A stick works like an artist's tool. And a dandelion can be a new kind of toy.

Engineers are **inspired** by nature too. When engineers work to make the world a better place, they often study plants for ideas. The inventions they come up with may surprise you.

Growing Greenery

Plants and people have more in common than you might think. Just like humans, plants need food and water to survive. Both need clean air and sunlight too. But plants need one more thing that makes them different from humans. They need healthy soil.

When plants have everything they need, they can grow. They use their roots to take in **nutrients** and water from the soil around them. They use sunlight to create their food.

Parts of a Plant

Flowers make seeds so new plants can grow.

Leaves take in sunlight to help make food for the plant.

Stems carry water and food through the plant.

Roots help the plant take in water and nutrients.

In a way, humans need healthy soil just as much as plants do. That is because people need plants to survive. Plants are more than pretty to look at. They provide food, shade, and shelter for people. Plants move and clean Earth's water. They also make the air we breathe. On top of all that, some plants can be used to treat diseases.

Creative Cure

Can a plant cure people? Scientists think so. Parts of the Baikal skullcap (an herb) can get rid of some human **cancers**. Scientists are studying the plant. They hope to create medicines that can do the same.

Grass roofs keep homes warm in winter and cool in summer.

Familiar Sights

Look around. Do you see any plants? You may see trees out the window. You may see grass on the ground. Maybe you have a flower in a pot by a window.

When some engineers see plants, they are inspired. They study how plants work. They often copy plants to create new inventions. This is called **biomimicry**.

Biomimicry inventions are all around us. You may even use some of them yourself.

Japanese Shinkansen Train

Engineers designed a quieter train by copying the shape of a kingfisher's head and beak.

This fabric was based on pine cones and helps keep people warm or cool, depending on the weather.

Inspired by Burrs

Velcro® is an invention that comes straight from nature. It is something you might even use.

It all started when a Swiss engineer named George de Mestral was outside with his dog. After a while, he saw **burrs** had stuck to his dog's fur. He looked closer. The ends of the burrs had tiny hooks on them. The hooks gripped his dog's fur. This natural design gave him an idea.

De Mestral created a product that works the same way. One side is made of hooks. The other side is made of loops. This product is now known as Velcro.

Burdock burrs have tiny hooks on the ends of their spines.

This close-up image shows Velcro's hooks and loops.

This caretaker tightens the Velcro strap on a horse hoof protector.

Inspired by Lotus Leaves

You may have seen buildings with solar panels. But the panels will not work well if they get dirty. Engineers solved this problem by looking to nature. They studied lotus leaves. They learned water rolls off the leaves. The water takes dirt with it. Then, engineers made a coating like lotus leaves that would keep solar panels clean.

Leaves may be used for more than just staying clean. A British engineer named Wanda Lewis is studying leaves. She knows how strong they are in extreme weather. She believes she can use leaves to make stronger bridges too.

Arts

Put to the Test

Lewis looked at how leaves have natural shapes that curve on their own. Lewis froze a piece of fabric in this shape. Then she used it as a model bridge. The bridge stayed strong even when weight was added to it. This proved that natural shapes are strong.

Lotus leaves and flowers stay clean, even in dirty water.

This coated solar panel stays clean during different types of weather.

Beyond Everyday Life

People use plants to solve some very big problems. For example, **drought** is common in some areas. When there is not enough rain, plants die. That leads to a lack of food.

Students at the School of the Art Institute of Chicago worked on this problem. They studied cacti. Some cacti can collect and store water from fog. The students created a product that can do the same thing. It can help bring water to dry areas.

The thorns on prickly pear cacti gather water from fog.

Students created this product to collect and store water from fog.

Water is hard to find during a drought. You can save extra water by giving it to plants instead of pouring it down the drain.

Under the Sea

Engineers do not just look on land for ideas. Some look to the oceans too. Scientists in Wales found a special seaweed. It stops **bacteria** from causing a disease called cholera (KAH-luh-ruh). But it does not kill the bacteria.

Some treatments kill bacteria to stop them from causing diseases. When this happens, diseases change. They can fight back. The treatments will stop working. Scientists want to use what they have learned from this plant. They hope to find new ways to stop diseases without killing bacteria.

Scientist Forest Rohwer collects ocean water, so he can study underwater bacteria.

seaweed farm in Tanzania

The bacteria that cause cholera are most often found in dirty food and water.

19

Out in Space

Plants do not just help life on Earth—they go beyond Earth too. Scientists want to learn more about space. But taking photos in space can be hard. The sun and stars give off a lot of light, which can ruin photos.

Engineers designed a device called starshade to help with this problem. Starshade is shaped like a sunflower. If it is built, it would fly in front of cameras in space. The device would block light from the sun and stars. Starshade would use its petals to make shadows. This would help take pictures in space without a glare.

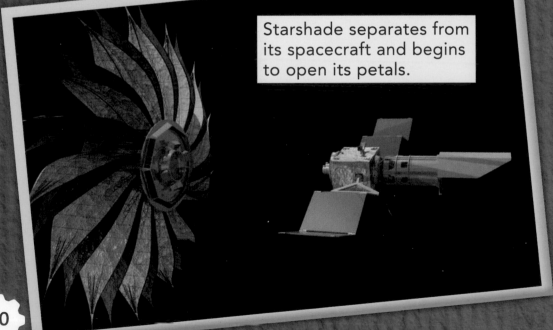

Starshade separates from its spacecraft and begins to open its petals.

Starshade blocks light from the sun and stars.

A camera on a telescope takes pictures in space.

Helping Each Other

Plants give a lot to our world. But people give back to plants too. They can help them grow and stay healthy. For example, flowers use pollen to make new plants. Wind, insects, and animals move pollen. This is called **pollination**. But what if nature cannot do the job?

Engineers have found ways for people to help. People can move pollen by hand. Or, they can use machines to blow pollen on crops. This process is called **artificial** pollination. It is a way of making sure new plants will grow.

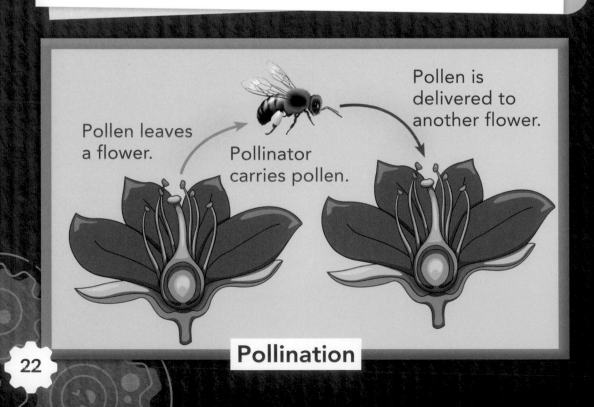

Pollen leaves a flower.

Pollinator carries pollen.

Pollen is delivered to another flower.

Pollination

These are small hairs (like on a bee), which grab and hold pollen.

Technology & Engineering

Robots to the Rescue

Many types of bees have started dying in recent years. This is a big problem. Plants need bees to spread pollen. So, a researcher named Eijiro Miyako decided to help. He created tiny remote-controlled machines to help. They can fly and pollinate plants in place of bees.

Engineers help plants in other ways. They often make models of plants on computers. They use these models to learn more about real plants. They can try new things without harming real plants. Then, they can teach people how to care for their plants.

Engineers have saved many plants with these models. For instance, they have found that electricity might stop roses from blooming. That could save a lot of plants when it is too hot or cold for them to grow. Then, when the time is right, they could stop sending electricity to plants. The plants could bloom and grow safely.

Computer models make plants easier for engineers to study.

This field of corn was tested as a computer model before it was planted.

Mathematics

Making Models

Real plants may take weeks to grow. Engineers can build computer models of plants in seconds. They use data from real plants to build their models. For example, they measure the heights of plants and the sizes of their leaves. That keeps their models as close to real plants as possible.

Partnering with Plants

People and plants work well together. We can help plants grow and stay healthy. And plants can do the same for us. We can find new ways to use plants. Plants can inspire engineers and anyone else with creative minds.

Inventions based in nature help people. People have a relationship with plants that is always growing. As that relationship grows, engineers can improve our world for both people and plants.

Engineer Masaki Otsuka was inspired by butterflies' wings when he designed this fan.

People in Milan, Italy, use plants to keep their buildings quiet and cool.

Scientists sketch and study plants for new ideas.

STEAM CHALLENGE

Define the Problem

You have been asked to build a model of a bridge. Your bridge must be built to look or act like something in nature. It must be able to stand on its own and support weight.

Constraints: Your bridge must only use things that are found in nature, such as leaves, flowers, and twigs.

Criteria: Your bridge must support five washers for one minute.

Research and Brainstorm

What is biomimicry? How has nature inspired new ideas? What natural items might make your bridge strong enough to support weight?

Design and Build

Sketch the design of your bridge. What purpose will each part serve? What materials will work best? Build the model.

Test and Improve

Place five washers anywhere on your bridge. Let them stay for one minute. Did your bridge work? How can you improve it? Improve your design and try again.

Reflect and Share

Which materials were the strongest? What items can you add to make your bridge more successful? How might your design change if it needed to be waterproof?

Glossary

artificial—created or caused by people

bacteria—tiny living things that can cause diseases

biomimicry—the design and production of things based on nature

burrs—rough coverings of seeds or nuts that often have small hooks

cancers—types of serious diseases that can spread to many parts of the body

drought—a long period of time in which there is very little rain

engineer—a person who uses science to design solutions for problems and needs

inspired—given ideas about what to do or make

nutrients—substances that plants, people, and animals need to live and grow

pollination—the transfer of pollen from one plant to another

Index

bacteria, 18–19

biomimicry, 10

de Mestral, George, 12

Lewis, Wanda, 14

lotus leaves, 14–15

pollination, 22

seaweed, 18–19

solar panels, 14–15

starshade, 20–21

sunflower, 20

Velcro, 12–13

Do you want to work in biomimicry? Here are some tips to get you started.

"If you love nature, spend time outside! Study animals and plants to see what you can learn." —*Cynthia Brown, Collections & Education Manager*

"If you like learning about plants and animals, then biomimicry is the field for you. Visit a museum, a garden, or a zoo to learn more about plants and animals." —*Gary Krupnick, Conservation Biologist*